HOW TO START
A SUCCESSFUL

internet business

Affiliate
Marketing
Guide

Starting a new business? Learn how to
get started and how to succeed.

CHARLES
WEALTH

About Author

I'm thrilled that you've chosen to explore the exciting world of affiliate marketing with me in this book. My goal is to provide you with the knowledge, strategies, and insights that can empower you to create a profitable affiliate marketing business.

Throughout this book, I'll be sharing my proven techniques, best practices, and real-world examples to help you navigate the affiliate marketing landscape successfully. Whether you're a beginner looking to get started or an experienced marketer aiming to boost your affiliate income, I believe you'll find valuable information within these pages.

By the way, I'm Charles Wealth, a seasoned digital marketer with many years of experience in the field of affiliate marketing. I have successfully launched and managed affiliate campaigns for a diverse range of products and industries, driving substantial revenue for my clients.

I am also a renowned speaker and educator in the world of affiliate marketing, having delivered keynote presentations at major industry conferences and authored numerous books, articles and guides on the subject. I am really passionate about helping others achieve success in the affiliate marketing space.

I'm here to support you on your journey, so please don't hesitate to reach out with any questions or feedback. Let's embark on this affiliate marketing adventure together!

Table of Contents

Affiliate product promotion strategies, paid advertising methods, affiliate email marketing, social media promotion, and content marketing strategies

Chapter 1

Overview of Affiliate marketing

Affiliate Marketing is a performance-based marketing method, companies pay people or affiliates for directing customers to their goods or services. Both parties gain from the symbiotic relationship: the affiliate receives payment for their marketing efforts and the firm expands its consumer base. The coolest way to make money from blogging or internet marketing is through affiliate marketing. Once the hard work is done, you will continue to make money as you sleep. One of the earliest types of marketing is affiliate marketing. Affiliates advocate things and receive a commission when someone buys them.

This business concept is most likely something you have seen in the real estate industry or other sectors of the economy of the world. The term "affiliate marketing" refers to the same type of business conducted online in the modern world, where practically everything is digital. In other words, using affiliate marketing to make some extra money is a terrific idea. You can build an affiliate program to start advertising your own established business or you can become an affiliate marketer and recommend other brands.

This comprehensive manual will show you how to start promoting other companies as an affiliate marketer. We'll discuss how to get started making money with affiliate marketing, successful online marketing advice, and ways to increase your income. Successful business owners are aware that there is always more they can do to expand their enterprise. Finding a different source of income is one technique to advance the situation.

Important Elements of Affiliate Marketing

1. Parties Involved

- **Merchant or Advertiser:** The firm that develops an affiliate program and offers goods or services.

- **Affiliate or Publisher:** People or organizations that use different marketing channels to advertise the merchant's goods or services.

2. Affiliate Links: Affiliates use unique tracking links provided by the merchant to promote products or services. These links track the affiliate's referrals and ensure they receive commissions for successful conversions.

3. Commission Structure: Affiliates earn commissions based on specific actions, such as:

Pay-Per-Sale (PPS): Earnings are generated when a referred customer makes a purchase.

Pay-Per-Lead (PPL): Earnings occur when referred visitors complete a desired action, like filling out a contact form.

Pay-Per-Click (PPC): Affiliates earn for each click on their affiliate links, regardless of whether a sale occurs.

Promotion Channels: Affiliates can use various marketing channels, including:

Content Marketing: Writing blog posts, articles, or reviews.

Email Marketing: Sending affiliate promotions to their email subscribers.

Social Media Marketing: Promoting products on social platforms.Paid Advertising: Using paid ads to drive traffic to affiliate offers.

Influencer Marketing: Leveraging personal brand and influence to promote products.

The Affiliate Marketing Ecosystem and the Importance of Affiliate Marketing

The affiliate marketing ecosystem is made up of a number of important individuals and components that support the affiliate marketing sector. The principal parts are as follows:

1.Advertisers (Merchants): These are organizations or enterprises that provide goods or services and aim to sell them via affiliate programs. In order to entice affiliates who can assist them generate leads or sales, merchants use affiliate programs.

2.Affiliates (Publishers): Affiliates are people who work with retailers to market their goods or services. Examples include bloggers, website owners, influencers, and marketers. For producing leads, sales, or traffic for the merchant, they receive commissions or other incentives.

3.Affiliate Networks: Affiliate networks serve as a middleman between affiliates and merchants. They offer a platform where affiliates can search through numerous affiliate networks, sign up, and monitor their progress. ClickBank,

ShareASale, and CJ Affiliate (previously Commission Junction) are a few examples of affiliate networks.

4.Affiliate Managers: Dedicated affiliate managers are employed by some affiliate programs to help affiliates maximize their marketing efforts. They offer information, respond to inquiries, and support affiliates in their endeavors.

5.Customers (consumers): They are the end-users who make purchases using affiliate links for goods or services. They might or might not be conscious that they're taking part in an affiliate marketing exchange.

6.Tracking and analytics tools: They are used to keep track of how well affiliate marketing efforts are performing. They monitor clicks, conversions, and commissions to help affiliates and retailers evaluate the success of their campaigns.

7.Affiliate Marketing Content: Affiliate marketing contents include blog entries, reviews, videos, social media posts, and email marketing campaigns. Affiliates use this material to market goods or services. The effectiveness of affiliate marketing is significantly influenced by the caliber and relevance of this material.Affiliate

8.Links and Tracking Codes: Affiliates make use of distinctive tracking links that are offered by the retailer or affiliate network. These links include tracking codes that allow for accurate commission attribution and reveal which affiliate referred a consumer.

9.Payment Processors: Payment   processors are in charge of paying affiliates their commissions. Through a variety of payment options, such as checks,

PayPal, direct deposit, or wire transfers, they make it easier for merchants to distribute earnings to affiliates.

10.Regulatory agencies and Compliance Standards: Standards are established by regulatory agencies, such as the Federal Trade Commission (FTC) in the United States, to ensure honesty and moral behavior in affiliate marketing. Affiliates must tell their viewers about their affiliate relationships.

11.Reviews and Feedbacks Platforms: These platforms let users post reviews and comments about goods or services they've purchased through affiliate links. Positive feedback can increase an affiliate's trustworthiness and drive additional sales.

12 Forums and Communities for Affiliate Marketing: Online forums and communities give affiliates a place to exchange information, ask questions, and network with others in the industry. They can be valuable sources of information and support

A dynamic and profitable environment is created for everyone involved in the affiliate marketing ecosystem by collaboration between merchants and affiliates, enabled by affiliate networks and supported by tracking tools and ethical norms. To achieve mutually beneficial results, successful affiliate marketing efforts frequently need careful planning, focused content, and constant optimization.

Chapter 2

1.It is fairly inexpensive to start

Opening an online business can be quite affordable.As I mentioned earlier, a lot of small businesses operating online have built their empires using nothing more than a computer, a domain name, and a web hosting service to hold their websites and disseminate their information to the millions of users online.

You can anticipate spending between $100 and $200 (for the entire year) to get started, and with time you can start to make enough money to start creating a lifestyle that enables you to prioritize the things you enjoy.You can produce products and/or services to sell to your targeted audience once you've built a blog, company website, or online store, spent some time gaining traffic, and built an audience.

Because they can be produced for little to no money and are accessible for download 24 hours a day, 7 days a week, digital information items, software, and services are immensely popular among many tiny web businesses and bloggers.To help you build a product that is helpful to your customers, you can either create your own products, depending on your degree of experience, or hire someone else for more sophisticated tasks.

For those who would rather devote their time and energy to providing entertainment, information, and/or education than producing products, such as those who work as bloggers (in a particular niche), you have the option to promote goods from other companies and make money from each sale.

It's nice that you don't have to spend all of your time, money, and resources developing your own goods or services when you promote other companies' items as an affiliate.Simply give the greatest recommendations to others, and you can get paid for enlightening them about why a specific good or service is a fantastic choice for them.The fact that you don't have to ship any things and have access to a virtually limitless supply since everything is digital is one of the nicest aspects of running an online business.

On the other hand, you could decide to start an online store that deals in tangible goods and utilize your online presence to advertise and sell your goods to the millions of users that access the internet every day.

As opposed to operating a traditional brick and mortar store, this enables you to reach a far wider audience. Additionally, as I've already indicated, online stores are constantly open for business and don't need you to be there for a transaction to take place.

Another crucial point to remember is that you can launch an independent web business with little more than some time and labor. You don't have to worry about paying rent, workers, or other costs associated with running a normal business.With such a low entrance barrier, you can use your skills, knowledge, and experience to produce something that you can sell or trade.In reality, one of the cheapest enterprises for a solo entrepreneur to launch rapidly for many small businesses and content blogs is an internet website.

2.You have flexibility of your time

You may wind up having a lot more flexibility in setting a work schedule that works for you depending on the type of internet business you decide to launch. As long as you set up your business well, you may choose the hours you want to work, the days of the week you want to work, and the time of day.

This doesn't indicate that you can just unwind all the time, but it does provide you more flexibility in deciding when to concentrate on being productive, whether it's from Monday through Friday or just on the weekends, and whether it's in the morning, evening, or during the day.

your income is frequently based on how productive you are with your time and how efficiently your business processes function, rather than the amount of hours you work, you are not constrained by an hourly rate

Because your schedule is more flexible, you can devote more of your time to vital tasks both inside and outside of work. You can also find more time for the things that are truly important to you (away from your business).

3. Affiliate marketing gives you the freedom of choosing your location

Part of the benefits of affiliate marketing is that it provides the freedom to choose your location. Unlike traditional jobs that often require you to be physically present at a specific office or location, affiliate marketing can be done from anywhere with an internet connection.

As an affiliate marketer, your main job is to promote products or services on behalf of a merchant or company. This typically involves creating content, such as blog posts, social media posts, videos, or email campaigns, to attract potential customers and encourage them to make a purchase through your affiliate links.

Since your task is primarily online, you have the flexibility to work from the comfort of your own home, a coffee shop, or any other location that suits your preferences. This means you can choose to live in a different city or even travel while continuing to run your affiliate marketing business.

This freedom of location can be particularly intriguing for individuals who enjoy exploring new places, want to be closer to family or friends in a different location, or simply prefer the flexibility of working remotely. However, it's important to note that while affiliate marketing provides the freedom to choose your location, it still requires dedication, effort, and effective marketing strategies to be successful.

4. Affiliate marketing offers significant income and growth

As affiliate marketer, your main task is to promote affiliate marketing can offer significant income and growth potential. The earning potential in affiliate marketing is often determined by various factors, including the products or services you promote, the size and engagement of your audience, and the effectiveness of your marketing strategies. Here are a few reasons why affiliate marketing can be lucrative:

Commission Structure: Many affiliate programs offer attractive commission rates, often ranging from 5% to 50% or even higher, depending on the industry and product type. means that for every sale you generate through your affiliate links, you earn a percentage of the total sale value as a commission.

Diverse Product Range: Affiliate marketing allows you to promote a wide range of products or services across different industries and niches. This gives you the flexibility to select products that align with your interests and cater to a specific target audience. By identifying high-demand products and effectively promoting them, you can increase your chances of earning substantial commissions.

Affiliate Scalability: Affiliate marketing has scalability built into its model. As you gain experience and develop effective marketing strategies, you can expand your reach and promote products to a larger audience.

Passive Income Potential: One of the appealing aspects of affiliate marketing is the potential for passive income. Once you've set up your marketing channels, such as a website, blog, or social media accounts, and established a steady stream of traffic, your affiliate links can continue generating sales and commissions even when you're not actively working.

5. You can outsource your work

As you grow your online affiliate marketing grows, and you earn money, you can begin to outsource some of your work, hire contractors or even hire employees that can help you continue to build your business further.

While many people may prefer to do all of the work on their own being able to use some of your capital (that you earn from your business) to outsource some of the work you either don't want to do or in some cases can't do you can spend much more of your time focusing on the aspects of your business that truly require your time.

Outsourcing responsibility does often cost money so this is usually a bit further down the line, however it can help you significantly grow your business at a much faster rate once you're able to do so.

Usually some entrepreneurs attain to the point where they are able to continually grow their business while outsourcing the vast majority of the work, which offers them a lot more time and freedom to spend their personal time on other things they enjoy.

6. Allows you to focus on what matters most to you.

One of the flexibilities about starting an online business is that it offers you to focus on the very things that interest you the most (if you choose) and this can make it easier to sustain your efforts and maintain motivation while you grow.

However, other types of work where you end up primarily focusing on tasks that don't interest you, the work you do in your online business projects empowers you with full control and creative freedom over what you choose to work on and how you plan to achieve your goals

This also allows you to share your experiences and interests with other like minded individuals with extra income while also giving you the freedom to build a platform that you can grow over time.

Finally (outside of the traditional e-commerce website) many small online businesses, blogs and websites today earn a living by educating others and helping them achieve their own goals.

Chapter 3

Benefits of Affiliate Marketing

Starting out doesn't cost anything; in fact, most of the programs that accomplish this will be open to anyone. Therefore, if you have any expenses, they will likely be related to the marketing and referral strategies you select, over which you have some control.

2. The product or service does not have to be made by you personally. All that remains is to advertise it.

3. You won't need to ship any products or hold any inventory on hand.

4. As long as your workplace has internet connectivity, you can choose the time of day you wish to work and the location of your office.

5. Possibility of passive income once your firm has gained traction. How effectively you market your affiliate programs will determine this.

6. You can include it into an existing home business to add another source of revenue. For coaches, bloggers, information entrepreneurs, and anyone with a website, this can be excellent.

Chapter 4

Challenges of Affiliate Marketing

While affiliate marketing has many positive aspects and often works well for users, there are some situations in which it might not be the ideal choice for you. Working in affiliate marketing can be challenging, and you may need to put in more effort than you had anticipated before seeing any progress. The following are a few drawbacks to affiliate marketing that may discourage some people:

1 .Creating the appropriate volume of traffic necessary to earn money can take a lot of time.

2. Sometimes a practice known as affiliate hijacking takes place. You don't get credit for some of your referrals. When this happens, You can solve this problem by using URL masking so that you genuinely get compensated for the clicks and referrals you make.

3. Your credibility can be severely harmed by an unreliable affiliate recommendation. To avoid having to later win back your audience and their trust, you must carefully consider your options and choose an affiliate quickly. You

4. You won't be able to influence the company's offerings, including the goods they sell and the services they offer, or how they handle them.

5. There some businesses are infamous for failing to pay their affiliates. To guarantee that you choose the appropriate business, you must screen everybody you intend to work with.

6. There is fierce rivalry. You will find that there are many other people who want to join it as well when you do find a decent program that pays you well and has a good product.

7. The consumer will be the retailer's property. Your statistic will reveal how many of each product were sold.

However, you won't typically get any details about who is buying the merchandise. This makes it more challenging for you to proceed with any resale marketing.

In conclusion, affiliate marketing is a sort of performance-based marketing that depends on alliances between affiliates and merchants. It provides a practical tool for companies to widen their market and for people to make money by endorsing goods or services they value. The choice of a profitable niche, good marketing tactics, and continuing optimization are frequently necessary for affiliate marketing success.

Chapter 5

Every affiliate marketer is constantly searching for the lucrative market with the highest payout. Sometimes they believe there is a simple formula for it that they can use. The situation is actually more convoluted than that. It's merely smart marketing techniques that have stood the test of time thanks to years of effort and commitment.

There are strategies that have been successful in the past with online marketing and are still effective now with online affiliate marketing. You can boost your sales and remain competitive in online affiliate marketing by using these top three marketing tips. These three strategies are what?

1.Making each of your individual products the focus of a distinct web page for promotion: Do not combine everything in an effort to reduce your site hosting costs. It is best to have a website that only offers products, nothing else. Include product reviews at all times on the website so that users can get a basic idea of what the product can achieve for customers.

Include reviews from customers who have used the product as well. Check to see whether these clients are more than happy to have their names and pictures used on the website for the particular product you are marketing. As an additional page on the website, you can also write articles showcasing the usage of the product.

Make the pages appealing and intriguing, and add calls to action. Each headline ought to entice readers to click through, read more, or perhaps get in touch with you. Emphasize your unique selling characteristics. This will make it easier for your viewers to understand the topic of the page and encourage them to read further.

2. Give your readers access to free reports: If at all feasible, place them at the very top of your website so that nobody can miss them. Try to write auto responder letters that will be sent to people that fill out your sign-up form with their personal information. A transaction is often concluded on the eighth contact with a prospect, according to studies.

With just a web page, just one of two things may happen: a closed transaction or a prospect leaving the website and never coming back. You can remind people about the goods they later thought they wanted and learn that the sale is over by sending them helpful information at a predetermined time.

Make sure the text focuses on particular justifications for purchasing the product. Avoid sounding like a sales pitch. Focus on crucial details, such as how your product may make life simpler and more fun. In the email, use intriguing subject lines. Avoid using the term "free" as much as you can because some older spam filters still throw that kind of information into the trash before anyone even reads it.

Persuade those who downloaded your free reports that they are missing out if they don't use your goods and services.

3. Obtain the traffic that is specifically tailored to your product: Just consider how many people will leave your website and never return if they have no interest at all in what you have to offer. Create content for online magazines and publications.

In this method, you can find publications that are geared toward your target audience, and what you have posted might just catch their attention. Try to produce at least two articles every week that are between 300 and 600 words in length.

You can attract up to 100 targeted visitors each day to your website by consistently writing and updating these articles.

Never forget that only 1 in 100 people will likely purchase your goods or use your services. According to the average estimate, if you can drive 1,000 targeted visitors to your website in a single day, you may expect to make 10 sales. If you give the strategies listed above some thought, they don't seem all that tough to execute. It only needs a little time from you and a strategy.

Use these recommendations for a variety of affiliate marketing campaigns. Not all marketers are able to keep a reliable source of income while thriving in this industry, but you can. Additionally, consider the substantial salaries you will be earning.

Chapter 6

3 Ways to Instantly Increase your Affiliate Marketing Commissions

Every affiliate marketer is constantly searching for the lucrative market with the highest payout. Sometimes they believe there is a simple formula for it that they can use. The situation is actually more convoluted than that. It's merely smart marketing techniques that have stood the test of time thanks to years of effort and commitment.

There are strategies that have been successful in the past with online marketing and are still effective now with online affiliate marketing. You can boost your sales and remain competitive in online affiliate marketing by using these top three marketing tips. These three strategies are what?

1.As an additional page on the website, you can also write articles showcasing the usage of the product.

Learn which items and programs to market. Naturally, you'd want to advertise a program that will allow you to generate the most income in the quickest amount of time. When choosing such a program, there are a number of things to take into account.

Pick the companies with substantial commission structures. Have goods that appeal to your target market. And they have a well-established history of paying its affiliates promptly and easily.

You should abandon that program and keep looking for other ones if you are unable to raise your investments.

There are tens of thousands of affiliate programs available online, so you have every right to be picky. To protect your investment in advertising, you might wish to pick the best.

2. Get the email addresses of those who download your free ebooks and save them.

It is common knowledge that customers do not buy on their first contact with a business. To make a sale, you might want to send your message more than six times. This is the straightforward justification for why you ought to get the contact details of readers of your reports and ebooks. Contact these people again to persuade them to buy anything from you.

Before directing a prospect to the vendor's website, get their contact details. Keep in mind that you are giving product owners free advertising. Only after a sale is made do you get compensated.

Ask retailers for a bigger than usual commission. A percentage commission for your sales should be negotiated with the merchant if you have already had success with a particular promotion.

The merchant, if wise, will probably agree to your request rather than risk losing a valuable asset in you. Don't be afraid to ask for more commissions because, to your merchant, you represent a zero-risk investment. Just make an effort to be reasonable. Create compelling pay per click ads.

Efficient way to advertise online is through PPC search engines. As an affiliate, maintaining PPC campaigns like Google AdWords and Overture is all you need to do to generate a modest living.

Then you should try to keep an eye on them to discover which ads are more successful and get rid of the rest.Try these tactics out and observe the immediate impact they have on your commission checks.

Chapter 7

Starting an Affiliate Marketing Business, Choosing Your Niche, Picking Profitable Goods or Services, Determining Your Target Market

Selecting a successful product or service to advertise, choosing your target market, and choosing your specialty are all important first stages in starting an affiliate marketing firm. Here is a quick summary of each step:

1. Choosing Your Niche: Pick a niche that you are enthusiastic about or are knowledgeable about. It will be simpler to produce quality material as a result.

Investigate possible niches to evaluate their viability and level of competition. Researching keywords and using Google Trends can be helpful.

2. Choosing Profitable Goods or Services: After selecting your specialty, look for goods or services that are part of affiliate networks.

When choosing goods or services to promote, take into account aspects like commission rates, product quality, and the standing of the affiliate network.

3. Determining Your Target Market: Define your ideal audience or target market within your chosen niche. Who are they? What are their needs, preferences, and pain points? Conduct market research to understand your audience better. Use surveys, forums, and social media to gather insights.

Tailor your content and promotional strategies to resonate with your target market's interests and problems. Remember that success in affiliate marketing often takes time and consistent effort. Building trust with your audience, creating high-quality content, and effectively promoting products or services are key factors in your affiliate marketing journey.

Chapter 8

Implementing Your Affiliate Marketing Plan; Establishing a Website or Blog; Producing High-Quality Content; and Understanding Affiliate SEO

Certainly! Establishing a website or blog, creating valuable content, and comprehending affiliate SEO (Search Engine Optimization) are all essential components of putting an affiliate marketing strategy into action. Here is a quick summary of each step:

1.Creating a Website or Blog

- **Choose a niche:** Select a specific topic or industry that you're passionate about or knowledgeable in.
- **Domain and hosting:** Select a reputable web host and register a domain name.
- **Website layout:** Using tools like WordPress, create a user-friendly and aesthetically pleasing website or blog.
- **Create necessary pages:** To gain your audience's trust, include a about page, contact page, and privacy statement.
- **Add required plugins:** To improve functionality and security, add plugins.

2. Creating High-Quality Content

Develop a content strategy and choose the types of material you'll produce (blog posts, videos, reviews, etc.).

- **Use tools like Google Keyword:** Planner to find relevant keywords and phrases associated with your field.
- **Produce informative content:** Write content that responds to the wants and inquiries of your audience and is useful, interesting, and relevant.

- **Visuals:** To improve the appeal of your information, incorporate pictures, infographics, and videos.
- **Consistency:** To keep your audience interested, stick to a regular publication schedule.

3. Understanding Affiliate SEO On-page SEO: Make your content search engine friendly by incorporating pertinent keywords into the material's titles, headings, and body.

- **Link building:** To increase the authority of your website, create high-quality backlinks from reliable sources.
- **Technical SEO:** Make sure your website is secure with HTTPS, has a quick load time, and is mobile-friendly.
- **User experience:** By improving site navigation and design, you may give your visitors a seamless and pleasurable experience.
- **Track and assess:** Utilize tools like Google Analytics to monitor the effectiveness of your website and modify your SEO strategy as necessary.

4. Your affiliate marketing strategy should include the following steps: Join affiliate programs that fit your specialty and offer goods or services that your audience would be interested in.

- **Market affiliate goods:** Include affiliate links in your content naturally, such as in product evaluations or suggestions.
- **Disclosure:** To keep your audience trusting, always let them know about your affiliate affiliations.
- **Monitor and assess:** Track clicks with affiliate tracking tools,

Chapter 9

Locating and Joining Affiliate Programs, Looking into Affiliate Programs,
Applying, Assessing Affiliate Program Terms

1. Finding Affiliate Programs: Search for affiliate programs in your sector or
specialized expertise. Search engines, affiliate program directories, and social
media platforms can all be used to locate them. Look into well-known affiliate
networks that host a variety of programs, such as Amazon Associates,
ClickBank, or ShareASale.

2. Signing up for affiliate programs: Go to the website of the affiliate program
and look for a "Join" or "Sign Up" button. Fill out the application, giving precise
details about your website or marketing strategies. Before applying, make sure
you meet any requirements that may be specific to a given program.

3. Signing up for affiliate programs: Create a strong application that
emphasizes your marketing plans, web presence, and why you're a suitable fit for
the program. Describe your experience and traffic sources honestly.

4. Examining the terms of affiliate programs:

Carefully read the terms and conditions of the affiliate program before signing up.
Pay attention to payment thresholds, payment methods, and commission rates.
To guarantee that you get credited for your referrals, familiarize yourself with the
tracking and reporting system.

Look into any limitations on advertising or email marketing as promotional
strategies. Check the cookie duration to see how long you'll continue to receive
commissions following a referral's click. To maximize your success, keep in mind
that it is crucial to select affiliate programs that are compatible with your specialty

and target market. Always follow the program's guidelines and adopt ethical marketing techniques.

Chapter 10

Some strategies for promoting affiliate products, paid advertising, affiliate email marketing, social media promotion, and content marketing are as follows:

1. Affiliate Product Promotion: Niche Selection, Pick a product category or niche that fits with your hobbies and area of expertise.

- **High-Quality Content:** Produce informative content that highlights the advantages of the product, such as blog articles, videos, or reviews.
- **Product Comparison:** In order to highlight the affiliate product's distinctive selling characteristics, compare it to related products.
- **SEO Optimization:** To draw in organic traffic, optimize your content for search engines.
- **User Reviews:** Share customer feedback to win over your audience's trust.

2. Paid Advertising Techniques: Google Ads, target relevant keywords for the affiliate product using Google Ads.

- **Facebook advertising:** Place tailored advertising to connect with an interested demographic.
- **Native Advertising:** Consider native advertising platforms like Taboola or Outbrain.
- **Retargeting:** Implement retargeting campaigns to bring back visitors who didn't convert initially.
- **Affiliate Networks:** Some affiliate programs offer paid advertising resources and support,

3. Affiliate email marketing: Segmentation, divide your email list into groups based on the preferences and actions of your subscribers.

- **Create customised email** campaigns that connect with your readers by using the phrase "personalization."
- **Educational Content:** Before making a pitch for the affiliate product, offer insightful content connected to it.
- **Include a call-to-action (CTA)** that is clear and engaging, as well as compelling subject lines.
- **A/B Testing:** Test email components repeatedly to increase open and click-through rates.

4. Social Media Promotion: Choose channels, select Social Media Platforms: Choose social media channels where your target audience is most engaged.

- **Engaging Content:** Share interesting blog entries, pictures, videos, and product stories.
- **Hashtags:** To improve discoverability, use pertinent hashtags.
- **Influencer Collaboration:** Partner with influencers to reach a wider audience.
- **Paid Social Ads:** Consider running paid social media ads to boost visibility.

5. Content Marketing Strategies: Blogging, publish in-depth blog posts about the affiliate product on a regular basis.

- **Video Marketing:** Produce instructional or product-related videos. Offer free ebooks or guides in exchange for email sign-ups in the section titled "Ebooks and Guides."
- **Host webinars:** Podcasts to talk about the product or relevant subjects.

- **Guest Posting:** To increase your audience, publish guest pieces on other websites.

Keep in mind to abide by affiliate marketing laws and to be upfront with your audience about your affiliate ties. Analyze your plans frequently, monitor results, and tweak your course of action to achieve the best possible outcomes.

Chapter 11

Optimizing Your Affiliate Campaigns Through Tracking and Analytics:
Understanding Tracking Parameters and Performance Metrics

For you to be as successful as possible, tracking and analytics are essential for optimizing your affiliate marketing. To assist you in comprehending and optimizing your campaigns, the following list of tracking variables and performance indicators is provided:

Tracking parameters include:

- **Affiliate Link:** This is the special URL that the affiliate program gives you to use in order to track clicks and conversions from your referrals.
- **Sub-IDs:** To categorize and evaluate traffic sources or marketing efforts, you can add additional tracking parameters to your affiliate links. They assist you in determining the most effective campaigns or distribution methods.
- **Cookies:** The majority of affiliate tracking systems use cookies to link a referral to your affiliate ID. Understanding the cookie lifespan is crucial because it determines how long conversions will be credited to you.
- **Pixel Tracking:** Some affiliate programs measure conversions on the advertiser's end using tracking pixels or postback URLs. This makes tracking more precise.

2. Performance Measurements:

- **Click-Through Rate (CTR):** The percentage of people that clicked on your affiliate link after seeing it is measured by CTR. A high CTR suggests strong ad placement and copy.

- **Conversion Rate:** The conversion rate determines the proportion of clicks that successfully converted (e.g., produced a lead or sale). A greater conversion rate indicates that your audience is well-targeted and your content is persuasive.
- **Earnings Per Click (EPC):** The average revenue generated by each click on your affiliate link is represented by the EPC metric. To compare various affiliate offers and campaigns, it's a useful metric.
- **Return on Investment (ROI):** By comparing the revenue gained to the amount spent on advertising, ROI demonstrates the profitability of your campaign. A campaign has been successful if the ROI is positive.
- **Average Order Value (AOV):** AOV calculates the typical sum that clients who use your affiliate link to make a purchase spend. Your earnings may increase if your AOV rises.
- **Conversion Value:** This measure shows how much money you have made overall through affiliate referrals. It's essential to comprehend the precise financial impact of your efforts.
- **Customer Lifetime Value (CLV):** CLV calculates the lifetime value of a customer as a result of an affiliate referral. For long-term affiliate strategies, it is crucial.

3. Analysis and Optimisation

- **Split Testing:** Conduct A/B testing using various ad creatives, landing pages, or promotional strategies to see which ones are more effective.
- **Segmentation:** To identify the best-performing segments, segment your data by traffic source, campaign, or audience using tracking parameters.
- **Time Analysis:** Consider the hours of the day when conversions are most likely to occur. Adapt the time of your advertising accordingly.

- **Geographic Analysis:** Examine your audience's geographic distribution and adjust your campaigns to focus on areas with greater conversion rates.
- **Mobile vs. Desktop:** Determine if your audience utilizes mobile or desktop devices most frequently, and adjust your content and advertisements accordingly.
- **Regular Reporting:** To respond quickly to variations, set up alerts for important changes in metrics and create regular reports.

You will improve your affiliate programs, boost your earnings, and hone your entire strategy by keeping a close eye on these tracking variables and performance measures and making data-driven adjustments.

Chapter 12

FTC Disclosure Guidelines, Handling Affiliate Disputes, and Ethical Affiliate Marketing Practices

Forging strong relationships with your audience and abiding by laws like the Federal Trade Commission (FTC) rules, ethical affiliate marketing strategies are essential.

1.Guidelines for FTC Disclosure

- **Clear Disclosure:** It's important to make your affiliate ties known in a form that is understandable to your audience. This can be accomplished by placing a disclaimer such as "This post contains affiliate links" close to content that has affiliate links.
- **Transparency:** Always be upfront about the possibility of earning a commission if a customer purchases something using one of your affiliate links.
- **Prominent Placement:** Disclosures should be prominently displayed, as at the start of a blog article or right next to affiliate links.

2. Resolving disputes with affiliates

- **Communication:** If you run into problems with an affiliate program, get in touch with your affiliate manager or support first. Open communication can be used to settle many disputes.
- **Document relationships:** Maintain records of the terms and conditions of your affiliate relationships. When disputes arise, this material may be helpful.
- **Compliance:** Make sure you abide by the rules and regulations of the affiliate program. Account cancellation or disputes may result from non-compliance.

- **Mediation:** To settle problems between affiliates and advertisers, certain affiliate programs may provide mediation or arbitration services.
- **Legal Consultation:** If a disagreement cannot be settled amicably, you may want to consider getting legal counsel.

3. Integrity-conscious affiliate marketing techniques

- **Authenticity:** Always put your audience's needs first. Promote goods or services that fit your niche and actually help your target market.
- **Quality Over Quantity:** Place more emphasis on relationships and high-quality content than on maximizing affiliate profits. Trust and reputation built over time are more valuable.
- **User Experience:** Make sure that your affiliate marketing improve rather than hinder the user experience on your website or platform.
- **Continuous Learning:** Keep up of market trends and best practices to hone your affiliate marketing abilities and adjust to shifting consumer preferences.
- **Diversification:** Don't depend entirely on one affiliate network or revenue stream. To lower risk, diversify your affiliate partnerships.
- **Compliance with Laws:** If your audience includes users from Europe, in addition to following FTC rules, abide by other pertinent laws and regulations, such as GDPR for data protection.

Note that ethical affiliate marketing not only benefits your audience but also aids in the long-term development of a reliable and respectable affiliate marketing company. Always put your audience's interests, transparency, and honesty first.

Chapter 13

Scaling Your Affiliate Business Using Advanced Affiliate Marketing
Techniques, Affiliate Sales Funnels, A/B Testing, and Conversion
Optimization

Implementing cutting-edge strategies, improving conversion rates, and creating
efficient sales funnels are all necessary for scaling your affiliate business. Here is
how to go about it:

1. Innovative Affiliate Marketing Strategies

- **Advanced SEO:** To increase organic traffic, delve deeper into SEO tactics
  such as on-page optimization, link building, and keyword research.
- **Content Upgrades:** To develop a sizeable email list, provide worthwhile
  content upgrades (such as ebooks or templates) in exchange for email
  sign-ups.
- **Segmentation:** To deliver highly targeted affiliate offers, segment your
  email list depending on user activity and preferences.
- **Influencer Partnerships:** Partner with influential people or authorities in
  your niche to increase your credibility and reach.
- **Advanced Tracking:** To acquire deeper insights into your affiliate efforts,
  use advanced tracking tools and analytics platforms.

2. Affiliate Sales Funnels

- **Lead Magnet:** To entice potential customers to your funnel, create an
  engaging lead magnet (such as a cost-free guide or course).
- **Nurture Sequence:** Create an email nurture sequence to gradually
  introduce affiliate offers to your leads while educating and engaging them
  over time.

- **Sales Page:** Create enticing sales pages that emphasize the advantages of the affiliate product, including endorsements and other forms of social proof.
- **Upsell/Cross-sell:** To increase revenue per client, use upsells or cross-sells within the funnel.
- **Retargeting:** Use retargeting advertisements to re-engage visitors who browsed your funnel but didn't take the necessary action.

3. Using A/B testing

- **Headlines and Copy:** Find the copywriting style that best appeals to your audience by testing various headlines.
- **Call-to-Action:** Test different calls to action (CTAs) to see which ones result in the highest click-through and conversion rates.
- **Design and Layout:** To maximize user engagement, test various page layouts, colors, and design components.
- **Offer Types:** Examine various bonus incentives, pricing schemes, and affiliate offers to determine which ones work the best.
- **Traffic Sources:** Perform an A/B test on several traffic or advertising channels to determine which ones are the most economical.

4. Conversion rate improvement

- **Page Speed:** Make sure that pages load quickly to stop users from leaving your site because of long loading times.
- **Mobile Optimization:** To reach a larger audience, make your website and funnel mobile-friendly.
- **Trust Signals:** To foster visitor trust, display trust badges, security certificates, and privacy rules.
- **Streamline Forms:** To decrease drop-offs, streamline checkout procedures and forms to reduce friction.

- **Social Proof:** To establish credibility, highlight customer feedback, endorsements, and case studies.

Testing, optimization, and improvement must be done continuously to scale your affiliate business. To be successful over the long run, pay close attention to your analytics, try out new tactics, and adjust to shifting market conditions.

Chapter 14

Success Stories and Case Studies: Actual Case Studies of Successful Affiliates

In the affiliate marketing field, there is a lot of doubt regarding how many people are genuinely successful. I understand completely why that is. Anyone would be dubious if they observed that the only affiliate marketers generating money were those who sold tools to assist neophyte affiliate marketers in entering the industry.

You can understand why it occurs when you combine this with the reality that so many people are guarded with their knowledge and strategies out of concern that their niche will be appropriated and their revenues reduced.

You occasionally need a nice reminder of the potential success of real people. People that brag about their achievements, strive to uplift others, and don't care if their market is being overtaken because they are the best at what they do. I've located case studies from five of these effective marketers, and I'm presenting them to you today.

Just because you haven't established a foothold yet doesn't mean you should feel taken advantage of. Affiliate marketing takes time, to establish yourself, to build an audience, to create content, and all the rest.

Affiliate Marketing Case Studies Successful Stories

Darren Rowse

Darren is one of the most well-known affiliate marketers out there, and this is due to the fact that he is constantly transparent about his background, his methods, and his achievements. Even though he has had three more years to amass his success, It is still astounding. He had been doing affiliate marketing with Amazon for 10 years. As at 2013, he had earned close to $500,000 in earnings.

David McSweeny

David, a marketing and SEO guru from the UK, has 15 years of experience in the field. Based on his personal experiences, he offers his strategies and pointers for developing and expanding a marketing website. In just six months, the blog he cites as a case study went from being completely new to generating just under $4,000 a month. That demonstrates David's aptitude as an affiliate marketer and is astonishingly quick.

Hieu Nguyen Vietnamese

Affiliate marketer Hieu's story, while not as compelling as many of the others, demonstrates the possibility of an alternative affiliate marketing business strategy. He created an affiliate website, which he later sold for a significant profit.

Chapter 15

Affiliate Marketing Resources and Tools, Must-Have Affiliate Marketing Resources, Suggested Books and Courses

To support you in succeeding in affiliate marketing, these are some crucial resources, tools, and courses.

Resources:

Affiliate Networks, to start: To locate items to promote, sign up with trustworthy affiliate networks like Amazon Associates, ShareASale, ClickBank, or CJ Affiliate.

2. Website/Blog: Establish a reputable website or blog to use as a platform for affiliate product promotion. WordPress is a well-liked option.

3. SEO Tools: SEMrush, Ahrefs, or Moz are a few SEO tools that can assist with keyword research and SEO optimization.

4. Email Marketing Software: To grow and maintain your email list, use email marketing platforms like Mailchimp or ConvertKit.

5. Social media: Promote your affiliate links on social networking sites like Facebook, Instagram, and Twitter.

Must-Have Tools include:

1. Google Analytics, Track the performance and traffic to your website.

2. For simple website administration, choose a content management system (CMS) like WordPress, Joomla, or Drupal.

3. For link management and tracking, use programs like Pretty Links or ThirstyAffiliates.

4. Tools for content creation and enhancement include Canva, Grammarly, and Hemingway Editor.

Chapter 16

Emerging Technologies and Strategies for Affiliate Marketing

Affiliate marketing methods and new technologies are always changing. These are following trends and strategies applicable:

1. Using AI and machine learning: To improve targeting, create individualized suggestions, and spot fraud in affiliate marketing schemes.

2. Influencer Partnerships: Teaming up with content producers and influencers to market goods or services to an extremely engaged audience.

3. Video Content: Producing video content to engage viewers on websites like YouTube and Instagram, such as product reviews or tutorials.

4. Voice Search Optimization: As more consumers utilize devices like smart speakers, optimizing affiliate content for voice search.

5. Native advertising: Its seamlessly incorporates affiliate links and offers into content to make it less obtrusive and more engaging to users.

6. Data Analytics: Making use of sophisticated analytics tools to monitor user activity, conversion channels, and ROI to support data-driven decision-making.

7. Blockchain Technology: Using blockchain to track affiliate transactions transparently and cut down on fraud.

8. Chatbots and AI-Powered Customer Support: Chatbots are used to interact with users, respond to inquiries, and suggest affiliates.

9. Micro-Moments: Making the most of users' rapid mobile device searches for information or solutions to offer pertinent affiliate content.

10. Cross-Device Tracking: Creating plans to precisely track and credit conversions across several devices, particularly in an omnichannel setting.

11. Compliance and Privacy: Maintaining current knowledge of data privacy legislation and ensuring adherence to rules like the GDPR and CCPA.

12. Material Localization: Translating affiliate material for a worldwide audience into various locales and tongues.

13. Subscription Models: Investigating affiliate relationships with subscription-based services and products.

14. Diversification of Traffic Sources: Using email marketing, social media, and other traffic sources in addition to traditional search engines.

15. Affiliate Marketing Automation: Improving productivity by automating repetitive processes like affiliate payments and reporting.

Remember that the affiliate marketing industry is quite dynamic, and that since my previous update, new technology and approaches may have been developed. Success in affiliate marketing depends on staying up to date on market developments and being flexible.

Chapter 17

These are some important lessons to remember, an action plan for affiliate
marketing success, and several top affiliate networks to take into account:

Important Takeaways

1. Diversify your sources of traffic: To increase traffic to your affiliate content,
use a variety of organic search, social media, email marketing, and other
methods.

2. Make Use of Emerging Technologies: Improve Your Affiliate Campaigns and
Personalize User Experiences by Using AI, Machine Learning, and Data
Analytics.

3. "Content is King": Produce relevant, high-quality content that speaks to your
target audience's needs and interests. This covers articles about blogs, movies,
reviews, and more.

4. Maintain compliance with industry standards and laws governing data
protection to win your audience's trust.

5. Build Relationships: Cultivate strong relationships with affiliate partners,
influencers, and your audience to foster long-term success.

Action Plan for Affiliate Marketing Success

1. Niche Selection: Choose a niche you're passionate about and that has
potential for profitability.

2. Market Research: Study your target audience, competition, and industry trends to identify opportunities.

3. Content Creation: Develop high-quality, SEO-friendly content that includes affiliate links naturally.

4. Affiliate Network Selection: Sign up with reputable affiliate marketing networks (see below for suggestions).

5. Promotion Strategy: Promote your content through various channels, including social media, email newsletters, and SEO.

6. Analytics and Optimization: Regularly analyze your performance data and adjust your strategies for improved results.

7. Compliance: Ensure compliance with relevant laws and regulations, including disclosing affiliate relationships.

8. Relationship Building: Foster strong relationships with affiliate partners and your audience to build trust and credibility.

Top Affiliate Marketing Networks:

1. Amazon Associates: Ideal for a wide range of niches due to Amazon's vast product selection.

2. ShareASale: Offers a diverse selection of affiliate programs across various industries.

3. CJ Affiliate (formerly Commission Junction): Provides access to many well-known brands and advertisers.

4. Rakuten Advertising: Offers a global network with a variety of affiliate programs.

5. ClickBank: Has a reputation for digital goods and works well in niches like self-help, fitness, and health.

6. Impact Radius: A dependable platform with an emphasis on enterprise-level affiliate marketing.

7. Awin: Provides collaborations with companies worldwide and an intuitive user interface.

8. Flexible: Its offers include both physical and digital products and thousands of affiliate schemes.

9. Designed for SaaS and B2B organizations, PartnerStack offers high-value relationships.

10. MaxBounty: Recognized for CPA (Cost Per Action) offerings with big payouts in a variety of categories.

OTHER LIST OF AFFILIATE NETWORKS TO CHOOSE FROM

11. Awin

12. Ebay

13. Ebay partner network inc

14. skimlinks

15. Tradedoubler

16. Jvzoo

17. Refersion

18. Partner stack

19. Maxbounty

20. Webgains ltd

21. walmart

22. Pepper jam llc, etc